Mako Sharks

by Deborah Nuzzolo

CAPSTONE PRESS
a capstone imprint

Pebble Plus is published by Capstone Press,
1710 Roe Crest Drive, North Mankato, Minnesota 56003
www.mycapstone.com

Library of Congress Cataloging-in-Publication Data
Names: Nuzzolo, Deborah, author.
Title: Mako sharks / by Deborah Nuzzolo.
Description: North Mankato, Minnesota : Capstone Press, [2017] | Series:
Pebble plus. All about sharks | Audience: Ages 4–8. | Audience: K to grade 3. |
Includes bibliographical references and index.
Identifiers: LCCN 2016059067| ISBN 9781515770015 (library binding) |
ISBN 9781515770077 (pbk.) | ISBN 9781515770138 (ebook (pdf))
Subjects: LCSH: Mako sharks—Juvenile literature. | CYAC: Sharks.
Classification: LCC QL638.95.L3 B3475 2018 | DDC 597.3/3—dc23
LC record available at https://lccn.loc.gov/2016059067

Editorial Credits
Nikki Bruno Clapper, editor; Kayla Rossow, designer;
Kelly Garvin, media researcher; Gene Bentdahl, production specialist

Photo Credits
Minden Pictures/Chris Fallows/NPL, 17; Newscom/George Karbus Photographt Cultura, 9;
Seapics: C & M Fallows, 11, 15, 19, Masa Ushioda, 21, Richard Herrmann, 5, Rogrigo Friscione, 13;
Shutterstock: Alessandro De Maddalena, 7, divedog, 2, kataleewan intarachote, 24, wildestanimal,
cover, 1, Willyam Bradberry, 23

Artistic elements
Shutterstock: Apostrophe, HorenkO, Magenta10

Note to Parents and Teachers

The All About Sharks set supports national curriculum standards for science
related to the characteristics and behavior of animals. This book describes and
illustrates mako sharks. The images support early readers in understanding the
text. The repetition of words and phrases helps early readers learn new words.
This book also introduces early readers to subject-specific vocabulary words,
which are defined in the Glossary section. Early readers may need assistance to
read some words and to use the Table of Contents, Glossary, Read More, Internet
Sites, Critical Thinking Questions, and Index sections of the book.

Printed in China.
004704

Table of Contents

A Big Leap

A mako shark races
after a sailfish. The shark
leaps out of the water
to follow the fish.
Then it catches its prey.

The mako is the world's fastest shark. It can travel at least 20 miles (32 kilometers) per hour. Makos live in the open sea.

Long and Colorful

Mako sharks are slim. They have pointy snouts and tails shaped like crescents. The mako's large eyes see well in low light.

5 feet (1.5 meters)

11 feet (3.4 meters)

The colors of a mako shark stand out. Its back is blue or purple. Its sides are silvery. Its belly is white.

There are two kinds of mako sharks. Shortfin makos have shorter pectoral fins than longfin makos do. Pectoral fins help sharks steer.

longfin mako shark

pectoral fin

13

Hunting and Eating

Mako sharks are fast hunters. They catch tuna, mackerel, and swordfish. They also eat other sharks.

The mako uses its strong tail to zoom after prey. Then it attacks with its sharp teeth.

Most fish are cold-blooded.
Makos are warm-blooded.
This helps them hunt quickly
in cold water. The cold
does not slow them.

Mako Babies

Mako shark eggs hatch inside their mother. Between 4 and 16 pups are born together. Mako sharks live for about 20 to 30 years.

Glossary

cold-blooded—having a body temperature that changes with the surrounding temperature

crescent—a curved shape that looks like the moon when it is a sliver in the sky

hunt—to find and catch animals for food

mackerel—a small fish that lives in the North Atlantic Ocean

pectoral fins—a pair of fins found on each side of the head

prey—an animal hunted by another animal for food

pup—a young shark

snout—the long front part of an animal's head; it includes the nose, mouth, and jaws

warm-blooded—having a body temperature that stays about the same all the time

Read More

Barnes, Nico. *Mako Sharks.* Sharks. Minneapolis: Abdo Kids, 2015.

Meister, Cari. *Sharks.* Life Under the Sea. Minneapolis: Jump!, 2014.

Morey, Allan. *Mako Sharks.* Sharks. Mankato, Minn.: Amicus Ink, 2017.

Internet Sites

FactHound offers a safe, fun way to find Internet sites related to this book. All of the sites on FactHound have been researched by our staff.

Here's all you do:

Visit *www.facthound.com*

Type in this code: 9781515770015

 Check out projects, games and lots more at
www.capstonekids.com

Critical Thinking Questions

1. How are mako sharks different from most fish?

2. Why do you think people find mako sharks exciting?

3. What do mako sharks look like?

Index